became the World
Poetry Slam champion in 2012 and has been
the people's champion ever since. He is a big
fan of playfulness and vulnerability and tries
to combine both in his work as much as in his
day-to-day life. His poems have been viewed
by millions online, but he personally thinks
they are even better in person and hopes you
will come and see him perform live one day.

Details of upcoming projects can be found at
www.harrybaker.co or @harrybakerpoet.

*Harry Baker's way with words is entirely fascinating. His mathematical genius meets with the wonder of a golden retriever let loose on the beach and creates poetry which is completely unique, never clichéd and always guaranteed to take you on a personal journey. Only he can make wellies a metaphor for living life bravely yet openly flawed. His ability to see through to the very bones of life using the most random subject matters as a starting point, is mesmerising to me. This book will make you smile, laugh, cry and most importantly read things twice and twice again, to better feel the many meanings of his deep-dives into the soul. He also gives much insight into the art of creating poetry, lifting the curtain a little for the curious to learn more. A triumph Harry! An absolute glitterball, party buffet, plethora of a poetry and prose picnic. Do yourself a favour; purchase this book, then seek out Harry reciting his words, for that is when the magic really truly happens.*

Donna Ashworth

# Wonderful

## Harry
## Baker

Burning Eye

BurningEyeBooks
Never Knowingly
Mainstream

This edition published by Burning Eye Books 2024

www.burningeye.co.uk
@burningeye

Burning Eye Books
15 West Hill, Portishead, BS20 6LG

ISBN 978-1-913958-49-7

Printed and bound by CPI Group (UK) Ltd, Croydon, CR0 4YY

For Little Star.

I'm so excited
for all of it.

# Intro

*How long does it take to write a poem?*

This is one of the most common questions I am asked when I do school visits, along with *What is your favourite dinosaur?* and *Are you famous?*[1] I feel myself going into autopilot with my answer, saying that some poems come very quickly and feel very exciting, whereas some poems take a lot longer and have to be chipped away at, but that on average it's probably a month or two from that initial spark to something that I feel ready to share with people. At which point they gasp because, I assume, they have only been alive for a couple of months themselves, so that feels like a very long time.

I go on to tell them it's a bit like a musical instrument or a sport where the more you practise, the easier it gets. I then often lead a writing workshop where I give them about fifteen minutes to come up with something new, which in the context of the above doesn't feel very fair at all.

1    To which the answers are *Obviously a T-Rex* and *Yes, I am actually massively famous and you should definitely listen to my poems. It's weird that you even had to ask the question in the first place.*

While all of this is true, an equally honest answer would be *I don't know*. My first book of poems, *The Sunshine Kid*, came out when I was twenty-two years old. It was everything I had ever written up to that point and it coincided with me deciding I was going to be a full-time poet, which was exhilarating and terrifying and liberating and paralysing, and I had no idea what that actually looked like (spoiler alert: it's the second-best decision I ever made). It took me eight years to put together my second collection *Unashamed*, and it will have been just under two years from that being released to this little baby coming out. By this logic it will be six months before Book Four hits the shelves and you'll have just over seventeen hours to read Book Seven before the next one is on its way, which to be honest is quite stressful to even joke about.

But I have been practising. As much as I think every writer aspires to improve on a technical level, (and poems such as 'Ingrid' show I am as obsessed as I have ever been on that front), the thing I have really been putting the hours into is cultivating my sense of wonder. To not just be amazing but to be amazed. From the very direct action of documenting small things that bring me joy to the more unexpected challenge of finding the glory of God in postcodes, it is this intangible sense of awe and wonder that may not have modules dedicated to it in poetry courses, but that I believe is as urgent and necessary and worth investing in as any literary technique I have ever come across.

The other reason I believe this collection came together quicker than the last book is that I no longer need every poem to do all of the things all of the time. Gone are the days of three-minute poetry slams where everything I wrote wanted to be a bit funny, a bit clever, a bit meaningful and then a bit judged at the end of it. Each of the poems in this book has been given enough space to be exactly what it needs to be, and as a result it includes some of my favourite (and most varied!) work to date. From language nerds to pudding enthusiasts, I hope there is something for everyone, and more importantly I hope there is something for you. Perhaps it will inspire you to try to write your own poems, plan your own funeral, or just buy some new wellies. If nothing else, I hope it encourages you to practise seeing the world with a bit more wonder. In the meantime, I am off to get to work on the next one.

# Contents

New book, new me, right?

I love the ritual of a new year. A chance to look back and look forward. In recent years I have skipped the more specific resolutions to go for one overall vibe to guide the year by. Previous mantras include *Let Harry Be Harry, Do More Cool Stuff* and *Look After Your Big Rocks*.[2] This year's mantra was the slightly bolder *Be a Legend and Have a Great Time*, and, I'll be honest, the fact that you are holding this book in your hands is as great and legendary as it gets for me.

Despite this well-trodden path of not setting myself up for disappointment by keeping things nice and vague, last year I also made the mistake of adding in two ridiculously specific (and specifically ridiculous) new year's resolutions that then failed spectacularly. The first was to do a 5 km run the first week of the year (so far, so good) and then add 1 km every week (uh-oh) so that by the end of the year I would be able to run 57 km without even thinking about it. This was going surprisingly well until, at the end of a 39 km run in September, I injured my leg so badly I could no longer walk, let alone run. A planned weekend in the Lake District with friends soon became a trip to a garden centre so I could hire a mobility scooter and pretend I was in *Mario Kart*.

2    This last one was based on an elaborate metaphor at the time but is also solid advice for any budding geologists out there.

The second putting-the-mental-in-incremental resolution was borrowed from my dear friend Chris, who decided he would try to do one press-up on the first day of the year (so far, so good) and then add an additional press-up each day (here we go again) until he could do 365 on December 31st, presumably at the same time as I was running the equivalent of twelve laps of Hyde Park. I was so inspired by this mathematical madness that I thought I would attempt exactly the same thing, with the added twist that I wouldn't tell my wife Grace about it, and then one day she would turn around and be surprised by how unbelievably hench I had got, at which point I would reveal all. What could possibly go wrong?

Reader, I did not make it as far as September this time. While it turns out it is easy enough to do one or two press-ups in secret when your other half is in another room of the house, it begins to feel less possible when you remember just before bed that you have forty-seven left of your daily quota. When you find yourself excusing yourself to double-check the door is locked, going downstairs and panting in the dark for ten minutes before reappearing unable to physically stand or really even breathe very well, there's only so long you can go on.[3]

3     I mean *go on* in terms of the press-ups, but it possibly applies to the marriage as well. The high/low point of this ~~breakdown~~ fun adventure was having a gig in Margate on 11 June and attempting to do 162 press-ups at the gig *in between poems*, despite not having attempted any for two months prior because I had long given up on the daily targets. I ran out of breath, I ran out of time, and I had to finish on the street outside the theatre surrounded by people cheering me on like it was the school playground. I still can't work out if it is the best or worst gig I've ever done.

All this is to say that I have learnt my lesson, and I'm pretty sure the reason why I went so ridiculously huge is because I knew I wouldn't be too hard on myself ~~when~~ if I didn't achieve these lofty ambitions. Often, in our self-inflicted efforts to better ourselves, all we end up doing is making ourselves feel worse if we don't live up to these goals. As an antidote to this, I have come up with a list of achievable resolutions this year instead. It's been an absolute game-changer, and I heartily recommend doing the same. If you wanted to start with *making a poet very happy by buying a copy of his book,* you've already smashed it out of the park.

# 20 Achievable New Year's Resolutions

1     To have an unexpectedly amazing hair day.

2     To drop something and then catch it again before it hits the ground.

3     To decide what my favourite shape is. I'm pretty sure it's going to be a hexagon.

4     To work out the perfect amount of time to cook an Aldi hash brown in the oven. The packet says 18–20 minutes, but I would like to crack the exact science.

5     To tell someone what I do without it sounding like an apology.

6     To find a new musical act I love, or rather to let them find me.

7     To turn a sneeze into an impromptu beatbox session.

8     To pack swimming trunks on the train from Margate to London and beyond. To change into those trunks in the toilet on the return journey, then see how long it takes to sprint from the station to the sea.

9    To buy more drinks for friends and to let friends buy more drinks for me. It may feel like these two would cancel each other out, but there is in fact a net gain of both drinks and time spent with friends.

10   To give up on a book that I am not enjoying. To remind myself that the characters will not take it personally, and that, if I am four fifths of the way through and still *just trying to get into it,* chances are it may not be for me.

11   To cuddle a giant rabbit. I managed this on 30 December last year, and I am already looking for my next fix.

12   To go a week without showering. Instead bathing regularly in the sea like the glorious mermaid that I am.

13   To get on my bike without a destination in mind.

14   To sleep the whole way through the night.

15   To share something that isn't necessarily perfect, or even finished.

16   To be something that isn't necessarily perfect, or even finished.

17   To hug someone I haven't hugged before.

18   To make a good enough new friend that this isn't weird.

19   To fail at least one of these, and for that to be okay.

20   To have an unexpectedly amazing day.

As well as a chance to look forward, a new year/book is an excuse to reflect. One advent I was asked to write a poem on the theme of *comfort and joy*, and so in preparation I started making a list of little things that brought me joy at the time. This list not only ended up becoming the full poem, but the making of the list became a profoundly moving and joyful act in and of itself, so much so that I vowed to do the same thing at the end of the following year, this time keeping note of joyful moments as they happened.

Sure enough, the more I paid attention to these nuggets of joy, the easier they were to spot. I have since used this as a prompt in school workshops and love seeing what the students come up with. Not only have others shared their own lists with me after hearing mine, but one person specifically said they even went away and were inspired to make their own crisp advent calendar. If that is the legacy my poetry leaves on this world I am honestly okay with that. I have shared a selection throughout the book, with plenty of space for you to add your own in too; I'm already planning this year's edition.

# *Things That Bring Me Joy*

*Deciding to make an advent calendar
of crisps for my friend.*

*Deciding to make an advent calendar
of crisps for myself.*

*Crisps.*

*Stroopwafels.*

*Super Noodles.*

*Leftovers for breakfast.*

*How proud my teenage self would be
of how often my adult self wears trackies.*

*That sleeping, reading, and writing poems
can never be a waste of time.*

*Clearing my inbox.*

*Turning my phone off.*

*Being out of breath.*

*Crying.*

*Especially in films.*

One thing that originally appeared on my list of joyful things but has graduated to a poem all of its own is ~~doing a big wee~~ my wellies.

I finished this poem about a week after I had finalised the manuscript of my last book and then proceeded to tour that book for six months, only for everyone to ask me if the welly poem was in it because that was their favourite. I figured what better way to get things cracking this time around than with that very poem, and I for one am excited to discover what it is I'll write one week after this gets sent off that will come to completely eclipse all the time and energy I've put into this book.

This poem came after an extended period of not feeling able to write anything at all, and it turns out all that was needed to bring me out of that abyss was the humble wellington boot.[4] It was sparked by my favourite Christmas present I have ever received, which in itself was sparked by a rant I had had many years previous and had forgotten about. This poem comes with thanks to my former self, and also, more importantly, thanks to Grace for all things always, but especially my wellies.

And six months of therapy.

# Wellies

I love wellies.
That is a statement of fact.
Footwear designed for
making a splash.
No need for showing off
status or cash,
no laces or faff,
just – I like big boots
and I cannot lie;
these babies got back.

On first glance as basic
as paying your tax,
yet that's still more outrageous
than Bezos can hack.
They are sensible,
functional,
playful and fab.
Put them up against tennis shoes,
it's game, set and match.

They just do what they do,
no overthink to their thunk.
All sole and no tongue,
like a Tibetan monk.

From farmyards through to festivals,
so grand is their appeal –
the only footwear guaranteed to be
out standing in its field.
While veteran shoemakers may disagree,
I think it's worth a mention:
that's just a load of old cobblers,
so pay them no attention.

You could be winging it
or wanging it;
the welly is the one.
If you've got booties
on your footies,
chances are you're having fun,
'cause any welly-based activity
is celebrating life.
You don't wear wellies to a funeral –
though I might ask you to for mine.

They are a statement piece.
That statement is:
*I don't want soggy feet.*

And beyond that they can be
anything that you want them to be.

Wellies

So, to my godson,
who's got some
all covered in dinosaurs,
or my niece,
who underneath her knees
has nothing but unicorns:
as you grow older
and the world begins
to open up to you,
you might expect
that is reflected
in your choice of welly boot.

Well, for the ladies
who are maybe
looking for a fun design,
I have seen bumblebees or daisies
or some multicoloured stripes.
And for the fellas,
if you wanna make your mark
upon the scene,
the options are
a fetching black
or an incredibly
dark
green.

Because what could be more masculine
than blending in with dirt?
Like if you don't see me
you might not see
I'm filled with pain and hurt.
And if you don't conform
to gender norms
or just try to ignore them,
if you're anything above size six
you're destined to be boring.

'Cause if they're just gonna get muddy,
what's the point of even trying?
Why have dreams when, just like us,
they're only gonna end up dying?
If you never dip your toe in
then there's no concern with drying.
Who needs waterproofs
when you can simply
stop yourself from crying?

I mean, God forbid
that one might have
a form of self-expression.
Why not blend in instead
with one in eight
that have depression?
Why be happy
when you could be a statistic
or a lesson?
Why do anything, ever,
if it starts to make you question?

Wellies

If we protect ourselves
from all those risky things emotions do,
it can be easy to forget
that joy is an emotion too.
And so is grief.
So is heartbreak.
So is happiness and rage.
So is this whole spectrum
that we miss out on
if we don't engage.

And I am angry.
And I've tried
so very hard
to hold it in.

And I am lonely.
And I've tried
so very hard
to hold it in.

And I am tired.
And I've tried
so very hard
to hold it in.

But we are not wellies
made with an impermeable skin.

You see, it did not do me good,
stood in a field of deepest green,
when it's a basic human need
to simply feel like you've been seen.
So even if this world insists
it's safer to be duller,
I would rather take the risk
and live life playfully in colour.

Sure enough,
last Christmas morning,
wrapped up underneath the tree:
a pair of size ten welly boots
as bright and yellow as can be.
They bring a whole new meaning to
saving up for a rainy day,
'cause if the skies are grey,
I'll be walking on sunshine either way.

And when it's messy,
and it's muddy,
and I don't know where to begin,
I'd still rather be out in the rain
than trying to rein it in.
And if I ever go on Dragons' Den,
this poem is my pitch.
But until then,
next time you'll see me
as I'm climbing out that ditch.

Wellies

*Watching the Lionesses win the Euros.*

*Musical Bingo.*

*Only Connect.*

*Taskmaster.*

*Ted Lasso.*

*My yellow wellies.*

*A decent WhatsApp group.*

*My nieces.*

One of the ways I got into writing in the first place was through music. As a teenager I loved listening to the lyrics in songs, and in particular the intricacies and playfulness of hip-hop and rap blew my tiny mind. After starting various bands with varying degrees of success,[5] I released one rap album aged seventeen before discovering spoken word nights and realising it was easier to find my voice without three of my mates playing guitar as loudly as possible in the background.

And yet the love of rapping never went away. Whether it is the joyfulness of performing as part of Harry and Chris, or the unmatched attentiveness and intensity of a rap battle crowd, there is something about it that not only feels very cool but, more importantly, is inherently fun. This means that even in my recent poetry shows I haven't been able to resist including some music as well.

Many of those songs don't make sense to put in a poetry book,[6] but one thing that I have no hesitation about immortalising in the written word is my love for the grapefruit edition of the German wheat beer Schöfferhofer. It is fun to say, it is fun to write, it is fun to drink, and I can only assume that, in the same way that Bob Dylan's lyrics eventually won him the Nobel Prize for literature, these words will be recognised for their powerful literary heft in years to come.

5      High point: winning an award for 'most potential' in our school battle of the bands competition. Low point: not being allowed to enter two years later because there was actually too much potential and it wouldn't be fair on everyone else.

6      One because it is entirely in German, one because it is a falafel-based diss track for a radio DJ that would take an entire book's worth of context to explain, one because it is a garage track about Greta Thunberg and a particular misogynistic influencer that I daren't commit to print in case his fanbase learn to read and come after me. All of which I heartily recommend finding on the internet and listening to in your own time.

# Schöfferhofer Life

I ain't in the club
sipping on some Grey Goose;
find me in the sun
drinking in the great view.
And by view I mean
wheat beer and grapefruit.
Scene one.
Action.
Cut.
Then I take two.

Any other drink I say *nah*
like it's 'Hey Jude'.
Proof's in the palm of my hand
like I'm Jesús.
And if you don't stock it
then I hate you.
Okay, that's a bit strong.
Unlike

2.5% ABV.
100% ta-asty.
It helps get you from A to B
if A is *All right*
and B is *Bloody brilliant*.

End of the day
it is light and it's juicy,
start of the day
it's still nice and it's fruity,
all of the day
it's like I'm at the movies;
just sit back and
take in the view,
see:

*I like a Schöff.*
*You like a Schöff.*
*We like a Schöff.*
*Drink it*
*'cause it's*
*nice.*

*I bring the Schöffer.*
*You bring the hofer.*
*Put them to-gofer.*
*It's that*
*Schöffer-*
*hofer*
*life.*

When I'm facing
a big Schöff
I take a deep breath
like I'm Wim Hof.
Soon as it touches my lips
we have liftoff.
Sweeter than Biscoff,
waltz in like Christoph.

Taking a sip
is like Christmas come early.
Grapefruit's in it
so I will not get scurvy.
It's basically
one of your five a day,
and it makes me feel
some type of way.

Even the ö with an umlaut
looks like a face
that is shocked
at how good it all tastes.
A life without Schöff
could be a waste.
It could not,
but is that a risk that you'd take?

It's a bottle
of orangey pink.
Like a sunset,
but one you can drink.
It tops any list
like it's *Gone with the Wind*,
and I honestly think
it's a wonderful thing.

Schöfferhofer Life

*I like a Schöff.*
*You like a Schöff.*
*We like a Schöff.*
*Drink it*
*'cause it's*
*nice.*

*I bring the Schöffer.*
*You bring the hofer.*
*Put them to-gofer.*
*It's that*
*Schöffer-*
*hofer*
*life.*

I can't get enough
of Schöfferhofer.
If I have a cough
then I will quaff
a Schöfferhofer.
I could offer
David Hasselhoff
a Schöfferhofer,
and I bet the Hoff
would scoff a
Schöfferhofer.

Honestly, I love
a Schöfferhofer.
There is nothing
I would put above
a Schöfferhofer.
In the words of philosopher
Dietrich Bonhoeffer:
we must allow ourselves
to be interrupted by God.

*I like a Schöff.*
*You like a Schöff.*
*We like a Schöff.*
*Drink it*
*'cause it's*
*nice.*

*I bring the Schöffer.*
*You bring the hofer.*
*Put them to-gofer.*
*It's that*
*Schöffer-*
*hofer*
*life.*

*That I am on a mailing list for a company
that makes reusable baking parchment,
simply because I bought a small amount
five years ago.*

*They email precisely once a year
to see if I need any more,
and I still don't because
the original batch is just so reusable.*

A univocalic is a type of constrained writing where you only allow yourself to use one vowel for the entire poem. You can still use any consonants you like (otherwise it would be less of a poem and more of a sound), and you can of course use your chosen vowel more than once (otherwise it would be a very short poem indeed). This form was initially explored by a group of French writers and mathematicians called the Oulipo, and taken to its natural evolution sixty years later by a group of artists called Joel and Harry Baker as part of an exhibition they decided to put on in Margate during lockdown when live performance wasn't possible. This particular univocalic uses the letter I, and starts off in the birthplace of so many creative constraints: a school disco.

# Ingrid

i

St Philip's. 6pm.
Mr Smith is spinning discs.
Mrs Sills brings nibbly bits:
crisps,
dips,
pick 'n' mix,
mini fish 'n' chips,
Lidl's pink stripy rings,
fizzy drinks.
I'm thinking
*this is sick.*

I spy with my tiny iris:
Ingrid.
Ingrid is Finnish, I think.
Whitish trim,
Viking skin,
stylish kicks,
I'm in bits.
My skin is tingling;
why is this shirt itchy?
This isn't simply shy –
I'm bricking it.

I timidly try...
*Hi.*
*...Hi.*

I'm sipping my milk – slick.
It slips - I'm livid.
My iris is filling with drips;
it stings.
Ingrid chips in:
*Why cry? It's spilt milk.*
I'm dying.
Wishing invisibility hits,
minimising this cringing fit.
Still – Ingrid is kind.
Insisting I trick my mind,
Ingrid grins impishly:
*Try this...*

Mr Smith is killing it.
In this jiffy Ingrid is singing:
*It's tricky, I stick this rhyming,*
*Stick this rhyming with this timing,*
*Tricky!*

Ingrid's lyricism is iffy;
still – it is brimming with spirit.
I find I'm smiling.
I dry my skin.
I'm chiming in:
*It's tricky! Tricky! Tricky! Tricky!*

Ingrid

DJ Smithy's still blitzing it:
P!nk, *NSYNC, Chic, City High,
DJ Zinc, Limp Bizkit, Will Smith.
Ingrid spits 'Jiggy Wit It' with vim.
I pitch in with:
*If I'm dying in my kip,*
*I think in this sky I will kickflip!*

Ingrid thinks this is silly;
still – I'm giddy.
My grin is sky-high,
thinking this night's limit is infinity.
My mind is spinning.
I'm slightly dizzy.

Mr Smith brings it in with
Billy J's tinkling riffs.
Lighting shifts.
Slight dimming.
Twinning is implicit;
it's simply physics –
I find this thrilling.

Will this bring my first kiss?
I'm chill;
still – if Ingrid is thinking it...
Big if.
I'm tilting in.
Lips inching;
Ingrid is...
High-fiving it is!
Ingrid sighs:
*Ricky – I'm...*
*flying this night.*
*I did my trip with St Philip's.*
*My British visit will... finish.*
(Wry smirk – Ingrid is Finnish!)

I'm in crisis.
My knight in shining whimsy is splitting.
I spy Ingrid's iris brimming;
I chip in with:
*Why cry? Is it spilt milk?*
Ingrid sniffs:
*This timing is...*
Instinct brings this psychic link.
I nip in: *Tricky?*
Ingrid grins: *Tricky! Tricky! Tricky! Tricky!*

I'm smiling.
*Ingrid –*
*this night will stick in my mind*
*till I'm sixty-six with wrinkly skin,*
*spindly limbs,*
*virility dwindling,*
*visibly dribbling.*

Ingrid's gift isn't my first kiss;
it's this insight:
if I'm crying,
I'll trick my mind
with iffy lyrics.

Midnight hits.
Mr Smith spins his vinyl disc.
*Night night, Rick.*
*Night night, Ingrid.*

Ingrid

ii

[Skipping fiddly middling bit]

iii

I'm thirty.
Big city.
Living slick-ish.
Jim is insisting it's drinks night.
It isn't my thing.
Still, if Jim's twisting my limbs,
I'm in.

It's in this hip district.
Dingy-whilst-shiny-chic.
St Philip's it isn't.
I miss Mr Smith.
This DJ stinks.

I'm thinking:
Swift Gin,
*chin-chin!*
Irish *pip-pip.*
In my digs by twilight.
Will Smith film night:
MIB.
Hitch.
MIB II.
King Rich.

Whilst I'm splitting,
I flinch.
My skin is prickling.
I'm fizzing with this third sight.
I spy with my tiny iris:
whitish trim,
stylish kicks.
It isn't, is it?

*Ingrid?*

Ingrid

*That time I did a wee*
*that lasted longer than a minute.*

*The fact that I timed it.*

*The thought that at least some of you*
*might go away and try the same.*

While most of what I write is to be shared on stage with people, I love that my books are a way of crystallising those words into something tangible that you are holding in your hand right now. When I perform at a gig, I have some influence over how you might take in these words, whereas in book form I have no idea of where you are or how you are reading this (although I trust that you are doing amazingly; keep up the good work). Writing poems specifically for an art exhibition was another challenge altogether, and was the only way that this next poem would ever have come into existence.

This poem involves what is known as the Macao constraint, where, rather than only using one vowel, we take a visually led approach and omit any letters that have ascenders or descenders.[7] The resulting text is a poem that is particularly satisfying to the eye, and hopefully the soul and brain too.

7    i.e letters with sticky-up or drop-down bits, such as
b, d, f, g, h, j, k, l, p, q, t, and y.

# as

as iconic as romeo's romance in verona
as ironic as a racecar's reverse manoeuvre
as unseen as a raccoon's mascara
as curvaceous as orcas
as raucous as a macaws' caucus
or maracas in macarenas
or a murmur in a vacuum

as cavernous as music minus nina simone
as cancerous as science sans marie curie
as anxious as moses minus aaron
as morose as sonic minus a run
as unceremonious as microwave rice

as nonsense as anosmia
as inane as insomnia
as insane as monsieur macron in a river
as overrun as a nose in a sneeze
as unconscious as a masseuse's snooze

as ravenous as a raven's nevermore
as raw as a necromancer's encore
as on course as crows
as on course as snow
as sure as coarseness causes erosion

as sure as casanova was a womaniser
as caesar was a romaniser
as sucrose is in macaroons
as warm cocoa cocoons
as summer sees us swim in sun
as seven minus six is one
as umami in miso
as memories in nemo
as a connoisseur's assurances re: vino
as seams sewn
as seems so
as a rose is a rose is a rose

as crimson as arsene or marc overmars
as communism, arson or marx over mars
as massive as uranus
as suave as cervezas
as ace as venus or serena's service
as serene as a mancunian oasis

as evasive as nuance in eurovision
as naive as a manicure on a man in crocs
as scarce as resources in samwise's mission
versus sauron or saruman's orcs
as severe as vesuvius's venue insurance
as unanimous as vicars in communion
as masses amass en masse in mass
as voices in unison
as vows in a union
as excessive as caviar on venison
as venomous as enemies see sea anemones
as amorous as mezze on a mezzanine
as enormous as an acorn's ascension

as common an occurrence
as assonance in verses
as cinnamon in xmas
as cream on eczema
as wariness in news
as weariness in use
as room in a rumi verse
as newness in our universe
as wow
as now

as rare
as ruinous
as nervous
as numerous
as insecure
as onerous
as awesome
as erroneous
as voracious
as vivacious
as vain
as vicarious
as unaware
as various
as curious
as us.

*Margate.*

*Writing a poem*
*about my favourite sandwich*
*for my local café in March.*

*Getting paid for that poem*
*in the form of fifty free sandwiches.*

*Nine months later,*
*that turning out to be*
*a more reliable currency*
*than the British pound.*

This next poem is my favourite commission I have ever received,[8] and the ~~nerdiness~~ intricacy of the last two poems should give you an idea as to why I was approached in the first place. After performing a poem about prime numbers at a Christian festival, I was contacted by a family-run software company based on the Isle of Man whose claim to fame is that they were the first people to use postcodes in online address databases.[9]

As well as still being big in the online data world, their faith has influenced the way that they work, including donating lots of their profits to charity. Therefore the specific brief I was given was to write something that *makes postcodes sexy while also reflecting the glory of God*. I will be honest: I have never felt more qualified to occupy the middle of a Venn diagram in my life.

8      Closely followed by the one that got me fifty free sandwiches.

9      If I had to give a snapshot of my life in a single sentence, this may well be it.

# An Ode
# to Postcodes

Some heroes wear capes,
some come dressed in Lycra.
Some swing on webs
once they're bitten by spiders.
Often the heroes are
ones that we don't know.
Here's an ode to the unsung hero:
the postcode.

First trialled in Norwich,
they mustered up history.
Imparting knowledge
with such specificity.
No need for sonnets
or colourful imagery,
just alphanumeric
pure rugged efficiency.

*It starts with the area code.*
You might pop to Preston
for the good PR,
or choose to chuck Coventry
on your CV.
If you dwell in Darlington
keep it on the DL,
or head to Huddersfield
for life in HD.

If you wanna get online
take a trip to Ipswich;
an IP address
gives you all that you need.
Or, if you're in Belfast
and you need to bell fast,
I can guarantee
your phone line comes from BT.

*The next digits give you the district.*
If central Newcastle
is your fixed abode
you can always say yes to
*Is NE1 home?*
Catch me walking round Hayes
in a daze for sure,
getting déjà vu:
*I've seen UB4...*

Or this happens all of the time:
does a German reluctant
to solve workplace conflicts
in outer Herefordshire
go and see HR?
*Nein!*

Imagine if Frodo
had known Mordor's postcode.
The eagles could have dropped him off
and then flown home.
There's no place like home
for Dorothy and Toto,
but it could have helped show
where the yellow brick road goes.

*O Brother, Where Art Thou?*
would have ended quicker
if that question's answered
with letters and digits.
Even *Titanic*
could have been less tragic
with accurate geolocational planning.

It's like we're all Disney princesses,
white as snow,
how up to seven small characters
can guide us home.
They may not see through walls
or have super speed;
they just help you get to
where you need to be.

All of this founded
on strong Christian values,
enacted in every thing that they do.
As they've given to
hundreds of organisations,
there's power in people,
and postcodes too.

Jesus cleanses the sins
of whoever confesses.
They cleanse your database
of duplicate addresses.
Jesus fed thousands
and walked onto water.
They validate thousands of emails,
and that's also important.

Some heroes can fly,
some are quick as a flash.
Some become
weirdly obsessive with bats.
Often the heroes are
ones that we don't know.
This goes out to the unsung hero:
the postcode.

*How hard it was to think of things*
*when I started this list versus*
*how hard it was to stop*
*once I got going.*

*The thought that at least some of you*
*might go away and try the same.*

What I love about poetry is that you can write about absolutely anything and it can end up being about absolutely everything. I am fascinated by how working within a particular constraint can force us to be more creative and come up with work that we otherwise wouldn't have dreamed of. This could be the mathematically satisfying challenge of only using 'squishy letters' in a poem, or the deliciously specific brief of writing about postcodes and seamlessly shoehorning Jesus in at the end.

The following two poems also both started life as commissions, on the (slightly less niche) theme of home. The first was written for World Refugee Day, as part of an alternative dictionary of definitions for what a refugee is, designed to challenge perceptions and stereotypes portrayed in the media. The second was for the fiftieth anniversary of a festival called Greenbelt which I have gone to ever since I was a child and is coincidentally where I made the best decision of my life, so it has come to feel as much like home for me as anywhere else.

# A Refugee Is

The nine-year-old insisting
we read his favourite stories together.
Picked up English so quickly
he is his dad's go-to translator.

The eleven-year-old
who has started to learn the violin.
He is the strongest child I know
and yet of course somehow this works.

The three-year-old,
same as my niece,
whose eyes burn just as brightly.
The mum who gives praise to Allah
they didn't have another boy.

The dad who always asks me
how the poetry is going.
Tells me in Arabic the word for poet
sounds like the word for hair.
I tell myself that is because
you cannot stop us growing.

It is making sure when we go round
we always have an empty stomach.
Knowing we won't get away with saying no to food.
And coffee.
And more food.
And the best baklava you've ever tasted.
And nor would we dream of turning it down.

First time Grace said we were veggie
it meant we got given chicken instead of lamb.
Not complaining because it tasted incredible.

It is the one time we fried and ate conkers
because they looked like chestnuts
they have back in Syria.
One bite was enough to know
that they are not the same.
They taste like conkers.
We look it up on the NHS that night
and find out they could be poisonous.
Call up in a panic and say we're so sorry
we might have killed your children.
Being laughed at down the phone
and told not to worry;
they seem fine.
They've been through worse.

It's agreeing not to tell them about the time
we tried to make falafel at home.
It's cleaning the house twice
before they come to visit,
knowing they will still find ways
to tidy up once they arrive.

It's Grace checking they would be okay
with me writing this poem.
Them saying, *Of course we trust his judgement.*
*After all, he chose you as his wife.*

It is flawless logic.
It is Friday prayers.
It is Arsenal games.
It is let me fix your toaster.
It is a milk frother made
from a broken electric toothbrush.
It is passing your driving theory.
It is failing your driving test.
It is next time.
It is FaceTime.
It is playtime.
It is helping with the maths homework.
It is when can we visit you at the beach?
It is we are coming to London this weekend.
It is friendship.
It is family.
It is our favourite wedding photo.
It is just a snapshot.
It is just the beginning.
It is just
completely
gorgeous.

*Going into any Turkish barber
and asking for 'the special'.*

*Sometimes it involves
a relaxing hot towel.*

*Sometimes it involves
having your ear hair singed off
by a flaming pendulum.*

*Once it involved
having lolly sticks
dipped in molten wax,
shoved up my nostrils
and being told not to scream.*

# Home

~~Home is where the heart is.~~

*Home is where the art is.*
*Home is where you can be open-hearted.*
*Home is where your soul goes to recharge;*
*it is cathartic.*

Home is aged seventeen,
putting your mate Luke down
as 'hype man' in your band
because it is the only way you know how
to get him a ticket.
It is him joining you on stage
and shutting every song down,
because that boy is nothing
if not committed.

*Home is where the past is.*

Home is being the only person
tuned in to your brother's channel
at the silent disco.
While 99% of the rest of the tent
are singing along to ABBA,
he plays Dizzee Rascal's 'I Luv U'
and you are so happy
you might cry.

*Home is where there's always room for dancing.*

Home is changing into yellow tights
in a stranger's caravan.
Being given a piggyback
across the mud
before your first ever
solo performance.

*Home is where your potential is harnessed.*
*Home is where safe doesn't always*
*mean the same as guarded.*

Home

Home is when you started booking poets
for *Woken Spurred*,
feeling the need to say,
*It's a Christian festival,*
*but don't worry; it's not like that.*
Ten years later,
its reputation speaks for itself,
You just add,
*It's one of the best*
*poetry crowds you will ever have.*

*Home is where you spent the hours grafting.*

Home is Chris fighting to stay awake
driving from Edinburgh to Kettering
after three weeks of performing together
in a basement/dungeon.
The next day, when you play main stage
and they all sing your words back to you,
you wonder for a moment
if you actually crashed and died
and have gone to heaven.

*Home is where you celebrate the harvest.*

Home is coming back last year
feeling the lowest you have felt
and, before you've even started,
simply knowing you'll be held.

*Home is where the light outshines*
*the shadows life is casting.*

Home is where, after a heady mix
of fate and Crazy Goat,
you let your guard down for long enough
to share a first kiss for the second time.
You wake up the next morning
wondering if you dreamt the whole thing,
mainly because you have been dreaming about it
for the last two and a half years.
When you join her for breakfast
with her friends and entire extended family,
she plays it so cool that it will convince you that you have.
It is only on your way to the main site,
when she locks her little finger around yours,
that you know the rest of your life
will never be the same again.

*Home is where there's always second chances.*

Home is a Monday-night lift from a friend
all the way back to Margate.
She says, *We don't have to talk if you don't want to,*
leading to what is possibly
the most delicious nap you've ever had.

*Home is where it sometimes hits the hardest.*
*Home is where you're welcomed in regardless.*

Home is where we're only getting started.

Home

*The Bear.*

*Ms Marvel.*

*The Marvellous Mrs Maisel.*

*Sex Education.*

*Asking friends in America*
*if they have Sex Education over there,*
*forgetting to explain that we mean the TV show.*

*Following this up with the phrase:*
*'Honestly, it's amazing,*
*you just fall in love with all of the characters.'*

Finishing my last book and touring the show that went alongside it was one of my favourite things I have ever done. After a particularly difficult few years where I started to believe I would never be able to share my words on stage again, it was especially cathartic to be able to do it on my own terms. This included such quietly radical decisions as visiting local schools alongside shows, making free tickets available for every gig if people needed them, gigging on Wednesdays and Thursdays so I could be home for weekends, and not paying for a single hotel room because I was staying with friends, family or, on one occasion, a complete stranger I met at the gig itself, who then made me a packed lunch for the train the next morning.

It was therefore very tempting, when the tour finished, to go straight back into it. I love what I do, and I am good at it, and I plan to keep doing it forever. Yet despite this, or indeed because of this, I knew what I needed to do most was to take some time out from performing. To allow myself to write for the sheer fun of it again. To put my creative energy into more than just worrying about a ticket sales update coming through at two in the morning. To have dinner with friends and finally get involved in the five-a-side football WhatsApp group I've been lurking in for six months. To not just make a living but a life, or, as Robert Henri puts it, *to be in a wonderful state that makes art inevitable*. This choice to trust my gut and embrace the unknown felt as quietly radical as any of the above. So I made the shrewd business decision to take what I made from the tour and go interrailing with Grace for two months. Here are some things I learnt along the way.

# Things I Learnt
# from Interrailing

That tiramisu tastes best
when it is eaten for breakfast.
That lemon sorbet tastes best
eaten straight out of a lemon.
That there are lemon trees in Italy
that are grown from orange seeds.
Once the roots are strong enough,
a lemon shoot is grafted onto the top.
The next time somebody tells me
I should be grafting more,
I will choose to understand this
as letting somebody else support you.

That hexagons occur in nature
from circles being squished together.
That I can be physically fit
and mentally still fragile as ever.
That there's a chance
I may just be this way forever.

That it is easier to learn to like anchovies
than it is to learn the Spanish for
*Why do these olives have anchovies in?*

That my belief in having cultural experiences
is stronger than my belief in vegetarianism.
Especially when it comes to fresh fish in Corfu.
Or a bratwurst in a German beer garden.
Or a ham and cheese sandwich
in a bus station
in Bulgaria.

That you can't spell *funicular railway* without *fun.*
That the harder the climb,
the better the view,
unless there is the option
of a funicular railway.

That if you pay €130 for a bunk bed on a sleeper train,
you absolutely get your money's worth.
That if you pay €3 for a seat
in a compartment of six on a sleeper train,
you absolutely get your money's worth.

That a 30 km loop around a Hungarian lake
is a bold choice for the first time
you ride a tandem together.
And ultimately the last time
you will ride a tandem together.

That, after five hours of walking through the woods,
when the Romanian locals tell you
there are bears nearby,
it turns out just because they are laughing
doesn't mean they are joking.

Things I Learnt from Interrailing

That when an Italian hairdresser points to your sideburns
and asks if you want your eyebrows trimmed,
it is hard to know what to say.
His English is a lot better than your Italian.
When he corrects himself and apologises
that he meant to say sideburns
but just got distracted
by your massive overgrown eyebrows,
you will allow him to trim both.

That it turns out *aperitivo* just means
serve every drink with tiny snacks,
and it is perfect.
That a 10,000 km pilgrimage
for a Portuguese custard tart
is entirely worth it.

That the food I will miss most
will be McCoy's salt and vinegar crisps,
Thai sweet chilli Sensations
and Nice 'n' Spicy Nik Naks.
That most crisps in Europe
are simply 'original' flavour,
which, when you think about it,
isn't very original at all.

That, when a gig in Romania
offers travel expenses,
they don't necessarily mean
a two-month Interrail pass.
But it is worth a try.
That it is always worth a try.

That on your first morning in Cologne,
when a man named Christophe tells you he quit his job
to set up a clothes shop because
*you have to live your life,*
it will be the most pragmatic
and profound thing you hear all trip.
And almost definitely the most German.

That you can meet up with an old school friend
for the sole reason that you are both in the same city,
even though you lived in the same city back home for six years
and never found the time.

That you can't lick the walls in a salt mine.
But also you can't not.

That no matter how scenic a view is from a train window,
sometimes nothing is as beautiful as a nap.

That when you comment on
how every place you stay in
has an incredible shower,
at some point you have to accept that
it might just be that your shower back home
isn't very good.

That you can get from Barcelona to Margate by train in a day.
That as long as I have a poem to be getting on with,
I'm okay.

That even when your final journey home
is delayed by a further hour,
when the café opposite the station
serves a crème brûlée the size of your face,
you will find it is impossible not to smile.

Things I Learnt from Interrailing

That you thought this was something you could only do
when you were twenty-one and carefree,
but it turns out you can also do it
when you are thirty-one and a bit wobbly.

That an instant camera might be
my best birthday present yet.
That days that start the worst
can still end up the best.

That not everything has to go in a poem,
but there is a poem in everything.

That nothing beats the feeling
of crying with laughter.

That fireflies are real
and they are actually made of magic.

That sometimes it is impossible not to smile.

That it is always worth a try.

That you have to live your life.

*Deciding to reframe the fact
that I often wake up in the night
as just being so good at sleeping
that I get it done quicker
than everyone else.*

One of the joys of going away is coming home.

I have lived in Margate for the last six years and I feel like I bang on about how great it is to anyone who will listen, so it makes sense that, when someone was coming to town to ask local celebs for insider tips for an online travel guide they were making, I was ~~not on their original list, but one of my fans messaged them to say they should consider me, so I was called up as first reserve~~ contacted.

What was initially proposed as a ninety-second voice note of me talking about a few of my favourite cafés evolved into the suggestion that I might like to write a poem instead, which was a shame because I was two weeks away from having to hand this book in, so I definitely didn't have time to write anything new. By which I mean, inevitably, an idea immediately presented itself and refused to go away until I had put everything else on hold. It turns out it wasn't so much me writing a new poem as unleashing a poem that had been writing itself in me ever since I got here, and by eight the next morning I told them I was ready to go.[10]

10      I initially reasoned that it was far too late for the poem to be included in this book, but then we all remember Wellygate, so if anything it feels far riskier to leave it out.

Because the writing process for this poem was so much quicker than normal, there was no time for the usual crippling self-doubt to creep in, so I have leapt to the other extreme and thought: what if this poem comes to singularly define my humble seaside town for many years to come? As I contemplated this entirely fictional achievement with a drink in one of my favourite spots, I was horrified to realise I hadn't included it in my original list, and quickly went home to rectify this and then worry about what else I might have left off. With great poems comes great responsibility.

Think of this version as a director's cut, with a caveat that there will be something I have forgotten, something I have purposely left out to keep it just for me, something that will have closed down by the time this is published, and something new that will have opened up in the meantime. You'll just have to come and visit to discover these for yourself. This is by no means a definitive Margate poem, rather the first of many attempts to capture part of what makes the place I now call home so special.

# A Bed Shop
# Called Dreamland

It is seeing the sea
the second you step out of the station.
It is smelling the seaweed
as soon as you get within fifty feet of the Turner.
It is queueing up for the special from Pete's.
It is dough balls from GB Pizza.
It is Po' Boy being open
for two hours at a time
once every leap year
if the moon is full
and it is *worth it*.

It is TS Eliot being an anagram of *toilets*.
It is Tracey Emin having a seal named after her.
It is playing crazy golf behind someone
who has brought their own clubs.
It is the council clearing away a Banksy
but not your actual rubbish.
It is a drag queen called
Janet District Council.
It is a surprising number of people
being into crystals.

It is Dreamland.
It is a bed shop next to Dreamland
also called Dreamland.
It is going into Scott's for a screwdriver
and coming out with a table.
It is stopping for coffee in Forts.
And Big Shot.
And Curve.
And Cliffs.
It is the upstairs table in Xylo;
it is the secret room in Little Swift.

It is two post offices,
one and a half of which are about to close.
It is Daisy's deep-fried Babybels
and frozen Kinder Buenos.
It is the best trackie bottoms
that I have ever owned.
It is Shell Grotto.

It is Christmas markets.
It is marches for Palestine.
It is people.
It is People Dem.
It is the Everyday Racism Book Club.
It is community beach cleans.
It is the rise up, clean up murals.
It is the Haeckels sauna.

It is a New Year's Day swim in the tidal pool.
It is a birthday trip to the Crab Museum.
It is pretty much a whole day out
at International Food Centre.
It is Margate Pride being the best day of the year.

It is jumping off the harbour arm.
It is fireworks on the beach.
It is outdoor cinema at the bandstand.
It is how have I not mentioned the sunsets yet?

It is the Tom Thumb Theatre.
It is the Bus Café.
It is the Loop.
It is That Running Club.
It is *that* moment at the CAMP quiz.
It is Where Else?
It is We Are Here.
It is brilliantly queer.
It is where I plan to be
for many years.

*That someone has named their pet snake after me.*

*That that snake is called Harry Snaker.*

*That I forgot that this had happened*
*until my neighbour reminded me*
*and then I got to experience it*
*all over again.*

From one of the quickest poems I've ever written to the one I have spent the most time on.

When I started writing as a teenager I would choose topics that felt important to me at the time, such as dinosaurs, maths, and trying to fit in (as someone who writes poems about dinosaurs and maths). Half a lifetime later, ~~I still write about dinosaurs and maths because it turns out they are timeless topics and I was indeed a cultural pioneer~~ there are other things that have risen to the surface too. While writing and performing began as a way to entertain myself and others (and, let's be honest, Schöfferhofer shows I've still got it), it quickly became a way of processing the wider world around me, and I love the power of poetry to hold these more personal and vulnerable moments as well.

Something that has undeniably changed since I started writing is that now, rather than being an actual child, I am at an age where friends are starting to have children of their own, or at least think about whether or not that is something that they want to do. While for many this is a joyful experience, I have been having more and more conversations with friends where it feels more complicated, so I wanted to explore some of that side of it too.

# Trying

I have this friend who is trying to have a baby.
Although *trying* might not quite be the right word.

To begin with it just meant more sex and counting:
two of life's greatest things.
Or, as their partner put it,
they were no longer trying *not* to have a baby.

Which becomes
not wanting to plan anything
more than nine months in advance,
just in case.
Becomes
making the most of this Christmas
or summer as a two
because soon
everything's going to change.
Becomes
two parallel realities coexisting
the moment a period's late.
Becomes
focusing on doing the things
they can no longer do
when they do
have a baby.

Becomes
if they do have a baby.

Becomes
there's always next month.
Becomes
I guess we'll just have to keep having sex.
Becomes
feeling guilty about the one month
they were relieved it hadn't happened;
they were just really looking forward to
their friends' wedding in September.
Becomes
you wouldn't want them to be born
around Christmas anyway.
They'd just end up getting
loads of joint presents.
And who wants
to have to compete
with Jesus for attention?

And it is trying.
And they are trying.
But *trying* suggests
they could be trying harder.
Suggests
they are not trying hard enough.
Suggests
they are trying and failing.
And some say it's insane
to keep trying the same thing
and expect different results,
but they honestly don't know
what else to do.

At some point trying
becomes
aching.
Becomes
longing.
Becomes
praying.
And in some ways
it is the ultimate act of faith.

Maybe *hope* is the best word —
it often is.
Because hope still comes with doubt.
I'm just hoping that
their hope doesn't run out.

You see, my friend is hoping to have a baby.
Although *have* perhaps isn't quite the right word.

In German, one of my favourite verbs is *machen*.
It means to carry out, to make, or to do.
Because it sounds like *make*,
my German flatmate interchanged the two,
leading to glorious turns of phrase such as
*Will we make party tonight?*
To which the only acceptable answer is
*Ja!*

In English, you *take* a photo.
In German, you *make* a photo.
In English, you *go on* holiday.
In German, you *make* a holiday.
In English you *have* indecision.
In German, you
don't.

In English, when you finish work,
you clock off or sign out.
In German, you *Feierabend machen*.
Literal translation: make party-evening.
As in you decide when you are ready
to transition from work to play.

In English you *have* fun.
In German you *make* fun.
It feels less concerned with ownership
and more with creativity.
As I think we all should be.

What I'm saying is my friend
isn't hoping to take or have a baby.
But I think they'd really like
to make or *machen* a baby.

I have this friend who is hoping to make a baby.
Although *friend*, it tends to not be the right word.

More like friends.

There is the friend who told me four years ago
that they thought that now might be their time.
And then they hadn't mentioned it since,
so I figured that maybe they'd just changed their mind.

The friend whose partner isn't against it
but wants to wait before thinking of kids.
And yet her body is different to his,
so she is not sure she can live with that risk.

The friend who takes folic acid tablets every day,
to help prep for her bones to be strong.
But when you've been trying to be strong for two years
you can only hold these things lightly for so long.

The friend who would be such a brilliant mum,
according to everybody that they know.
They just thought that they would have a partner by now
and they don't want to do this alone.

The friends who both wanted kids for a while,
and both committed to try IVF,
but had to spend £25k privately
before they could apply to the NHS.

Because they are both women.
And that is the only way to prove
that they are trying.
But they are trying.
They are all trying.
And aching.
And longing.
And praying.

I have these friends who are hoping to make a baby.
Although *baby* maybe isn't the right word.

Because of course babies are cute.
In the way that kittens are cute.
In the way that miniature bottles of shampoo are cute.
But most of my friends that do have babies are exhausted.

And having friends that do have babies is ideal,
because you get to have a cuddle
and then give them back.
Without the paralysing fear
of them discovering new ways to die.
Or the fact that the only way they know
how to communicate is to cry.
And they have learnt to scream at a specific pitch
that cuts through to your soul,
and all you have learnt is a growing list
of things that you cannot control.
And I get that it must come
with waves of unconditional love,
but it just. Seems. Relentless.

And anyway, surely the best bit's the next bit.
Because you are not just making a baby, but a child.
And they have not only learnt to walk and talk,
but to run down the street chanting your name,
and if you do anything they think is funny,
they will ask you to do it again.
And again.
Forever.

And in any given situation,
they would rather play than chat.
And I will be honest: I am thirty-one,
and I still feel like that.
When they are at that age
they do not *have* fun;
they *make* fun.

Then I assume
you muddle through
the teenage years.

Until one day when they are
not just a child anymore.
They will say that
they want to be a doctor.
So they can help people.
And you will say that
that sounds like a good idea.

Then a few years later they will say that
they have changed their mind.
That they want to switch from medicine to maths
so they have more time to write poems.
And you will say yeah,
that actually sounds a lot better.
And way more useful to society as a whole.

And while you cannot possibly know how it turns out,

you will still be there when they cry,
and it will still cut through to your soul.
And you will have added to your list
a thousand times over
of things that you cannot control.
And there will come a time
where they no longer go
wherever you go,
but you know
so long as you can watch them grow
you will still grow.

And when they value creativity over ownership,
or maybe run a marathon every now and then,
you will know some of that is down to you,
and you will make sure they know
you are so proud of them.

Because you are not just making a baby,
or a child,
but a life.

I have these friends who are hoping to make a life.
And so am I.

Which at this point
maybe won't come as a surprise.
I guess the giveaway was mentioning
sex and counting in the same sentence.

And yet, out of all of the friends that I mentioned,
almost all talked about it in passing,
and only one of those friends is a guy.
And I have messaged about since, asking.
And for whatever reason he doesn't reply.
But I am trying.

I am trying
to talk about it.
I am trying
to hold it lightly.
I am trying
to not get my hopes up.
But I like
getting my hopes up.

When I hear somebody say
they are expecting a baby
I realise that is exactly what I have been doing
for years now.

When anyone asks me if I have kids
I say I have three incredible nieces.
And three amazing godsons.
Or that having friends with babies is ideal
because you get to have a cuddle
and then give them back.
But one day I would love to be the one
you give them back to.

And when friends do announce they are pregnant
I am genuinely thrilled for them.
Except for the one couple
who joked that it was an accident
and that they weren't even really trying,
when so many of us are trying.

And I secretly hope their baby is born
with weirdly big hands or something.
But then I meet them.
And they are perfect.
And I guess that's okay too.

And I am so grateful to the friends
who knew what we were going through,
and so were sensitive to us
when sharing their incredible news.
Especially the friend who, four years ago,
said they thought now was their time,
because now is their time.
Even if it means that when I message
he takes a while to reply.

But the best is the friend with a one-year-old
who she obviously loves to bits,
and yet she says she spends so much time wondering
what her life would be like without kids.
How it must be nice.
And it is.

Grace says the hardest part is the not knowing.
Being stuck in the in-between
of now and might-never-come-to-be.
The truth is right here. Right now.
I know that my life doesn't feel incomplete.
And, whichever reality we end up in,
I know I'm so grateful that Grace is with me.

And I still think I'd be a good dad.
But I guess there's no way to know.
At least I have made a head start
on the list of things that I cannot control.

And while I cannot possibly know how it turns out,

I have these friends.
And I have hope.
And I am already making a life.

Or at least
I am trying.

*Celebrating my billion-second birthday.*

*Having nerdy enough friends to know that they have done the same.*

*If you are wondering, it's 31 years, 8 months and 7 days (ish).*

Something else that is happening at this stage of life is that I am going to more and more funerals. Two of Grace's grandparents died last year, and I found it very moving to hear more about the full and rich lives of people who I had only met towards the later stages of those lives. It also made me think about what I would like to happen when I die.

# Sunflowers

Ideally I would like
a hundred benches.
Every single one of them
facing the sea.
If that's too much faff,
I'd settle for the one
somewhere in Margate.
Somewhere you can come,
and sit, and think, and be.

I don't need a fancy pot
to keep my ashes.
Just find a decent spot
where there's a breeze.
So the next time someone gasps
at all the wonder in the world,
a part of them is breathing in
a part of me.

At my funeral
I'd like there to be sunflowers.
A truly inconvenient amount.
For I too will have spent a lifetime
searching for the light,
and I don't see a reason why
that should stop now.

Wear what you want.
If it were me I'd go for trainers,
or wellies.
Something comfortable
and colourful to match.
For, as it was foretold
by the prophet Jamie Tartt,
dress shoes are for muggles
and for twats.

For the reading,
I'd like Erin's poem
about final moments.
Maybe this poem
should be read
for context too.
For the music,
nothing short of
a full-throated singalong
of my favourite song:
'Dynamite', by Taio Cruz.

For the food,
just keep it veggie.
For the drinks,
serve up negronis.
If I pretend to like them,
you can do the same.
For the wake,
if people wanna chat
then I am all for that,
but, just in case,
make sure a corner's
stacked with games.

Sunflowers

Don't let anyone apologise for crying.
It is honestly my favourite thing to do.
Just make sure everybody knows
how much I loved being alive.
The only thing that I loved more
was loving you.

Speaking of which:
if you are free,
then I would love
for you to be there.
But if you can't,
because you're dead,
that's not your fault.
To be honest,
neither of us
quite makes sense
without the other.
I still think
we'll die together,
like a cult.

And if anybody says
I have gone to a better place,
that is a kind
and very well-intentioned lie.
For there can be no better place
than in a room with all my friends.
Just promise we'll do this again
the other side.
Side note: let's also do this
loads before we die.

And by the time
it comes around
maybe I'd hate it.
I'll live for ages
and my tastes
will change with time.
But one thing that I know
I will always find amazing
is what a thing it is
to live a life.

P.S. Let's also do this loads
before we die.

The Mission Impossible films.

That the combination of
joy and grief in my recent poems
has led to me being described as
the Barbenheimer of the poetry world.

That it was me
who described myself as that.

But I am hoping it catches on.

This next poem started out life as an anniversary poem for Grace. As I started writing a heartfelt declaration of my love, I began to feel the familiar temptation to slip in some ridiculous puns. The more sincere the poem became, the more outrageous the puns that followed,[11] and soon the only way to preserve the sanctity of the original was to create a second sacrificial poem where these lines could happily exist without undermining any of the sentiment of the first.

And yet love isn't just the sincere bits. It is silly and it is ridiculous as much as it is heartfelt and romantic, and if anything it is the combination of the two that makes it so special.[12] In honour of this, I have combined my favourite parts of both poems in an attempt to give a more comprehensive and accurate summary of my affections.

11      In other words, for every 'Just like the letter Y, I want to end each day with you', there was a 'Like Pumbaa riding solo, I do not need Timon' ('to moan').

12      Also I was arguably more proud of the second burner poem than I was of the original.

# Sticky
# Toffee
# Pudding

Your love is old T-shirts
and songs I know the words to.
As soon as I am with you I feel safe.
You help me try to be
the greatest version of myself.
I plan to spend this lifetime
doing just the same.

It's like the floor is lava,
how you set my sole on fire.
You are sourdough and canal boats;
you're all I knead and moor.
Like the price of advance train tickets,
I love to talk about you.
Like sticky toffee pudding,
you are delicious and warm.

Like the voice of David Attenborough,
I can't picture life without you.
Like a reluctant rugby player,
I don't even want to try.
Like a rock climbing enthusiast,
you help me to feel boulder.
Like the fact Tom Cruise is twice my age,
you're always on my mind.

You are my favourite place to cry.
You are my favourite place to nap.
Our love is a supply teacher;
it can take many forms.
You're very understanding
when I dribble on your lap.
Like sticky toffee pudding,
you are delicious and warm.

In front of you is the one time
that I feel sexy.
Except that summer when I ran loads
and got really fit and tanned.
Then had a rap battle in September
and they said I looked like I was on heroin.
And yet somehow you still managed to pull it back.
Then, when a well-meaning Australian dentist
slid into my Instagram DMs to say
she's enjoying the poetry videos but, on closer inspection,
she is worried I might have gum disease,
you even made me feel good after that.

The furrow of your brow
when you are reading.
The nuzzle of your nose
into my neck.
The way your eyes light up
when you eat chocolate.
Everything about you is the best.

Sticky Toffee Pudding

The murmur as you start to
fall asleep mid-conversation,
or that I know you have dropped off
because you don't laugh at my jokes.
The fact that right now you are thinking
that can't be the explanation,
because when you are awake
you also don't laugh at my jokes.

When you don't know what you want,
or who you are, or what to do,
I know exactly what I want,
and that's to spend my days with you.

Right now everything's
about to change forever.
But, then again, everything always is.
Was it not everything changing
that meant we ended up together?
Whatever's next,
I know we'll never not have this.

When it's all up in the air,
we will learn to fall with style.
When everything's at sea,
I will be with you in that storm.
When we're coming into land,
just let me hold you for a while.
Like sticky toffee pudding,
you are warm.

*Getting a new duvet.*

*My local queer coffee company.*

*My friend Helen.*

*Watching things with people
who care about them.*

*Caring about people.*

*Letting people care for me.*

Before I had even written the first word of this book I knew what it would be called. If you were to make a word map based on every poem I have ever written, dinosaurs and maths would no doubt be right up there, but I'm pretty sure wonder will have snuck its way to the top, as it so often has a habit of doing.

After the mental health struggles alongside putting my last collection together, the rough plan for this one was to write some fun poems to celebrate coming out the other side and then have a fun time sharing those with other people, because, frankly, life is hard sometimes and fun is fun always and we could all do with a bit more of it. But it didn't quite turn out that way. For someone who once saw themselves as the Sunshine Kid, the reality is that the last few years have held more grief and pain and sadness than ever before.

While I used to believe that the difficult parts of life could be overcome with hope and optimism, or at least that if we gave enough oxygen to the good things they could outgrow the rest, I have learnt that the painful bits don't just disappear if we ignore them or wish them away, but have to be accepted and acknowledged as part of the whole spectrum of what it means to exist in this wonderful world.

Rather than the darkness undermining that search for light and wonder, it is what makes it more vital than ever. It has been the presence of death that has caused me to double down on my love of life. It is the being away that has given me a renewed appreciation of what home is. It is the puddles that necessitate the wellies.

These hardships do not just serve as a contrast for when joy does break through (and it always finds a way). Rather, it is the courage to be open and vulnerable in these lowest moments that enables us to connect with others on a fundamentally deeper level, and it is the richness of that human connection that makes me more grateful than ever to be alive and here to experience all of it.

*Being prayed for.*

*Being held.*

*Being warm.*

*Being vulnerable.*

*Being open.*

*Opening a packet of crisps.*

At the time of writing, Grace is currently pregnant. We had come to terms with the fact that this might never happen and had a bit of a scare very early on, so in many ways it doesn't feel real yet, and I noticed I had been protecting myself by not getting too excited in case something went wrong.

After a conversation with my friend Dave, I was reminded that, just as the joyful moments in life don't mean the hard parts no longer exist, the fear of something going wrong in the future is no reason not to allow yourself to be excited in the present. In other words, I quite like getting my hopes up.

With that in mind, I would like to end this book with the first of hopefully many poems written for the little one. After almost thirty-two years I still haven't quite got it all figured out yet, but, just like any poem that I've ever claimed to have written for someone else, this advice is a reminder to myself as much as anything. While I cannot possibly know how it will turn out, I have a strong feeling it might just be more wonderful than ever.

After all, I have been practising.

# Wonderful

May you always picture where you are
as where you're meant to be.
May you take in your surroundings
like you visited especially.
We all end up in the soil eventually,
so may you carry such goodness
that it nourishes for centuries.

May you see life as a show
and may the entry fee be empathy,
sat front row with an empty seat
for friends in need.
When you're on form,
be generous
and spread that energy.
When you're not sure,
be gentle with yourself
and don't forget to breathe.

You need not be defined by your many feats;
you are not a centipede.
There is a joy in doing something terribly.
May you share brews and bruises
and may you do this tenderly.
You are the most improved you
there has ever been.

Of all the words you'll ever hear,
remember these:
life is too short
to eat celery.
Life is too long
to feed jealousy.
Life is likely just the right length
to need therapy.

May you be seriously silly,
may you be wickedly kind.
May you be brilliantly dumb sometimes
and yet stupidly bright.
May you certainly have doubts,
may your weirdness be the norm.
May the coolest thing about you
be your warmth.

May you be powerfully vulnerable,
or at least mightily soft.
May you be a contradiction,
and yet at the same time not.
And, whether you are any, none
or all of the above,
above all, may you know
that you are loved.

May you understand
that it's okay to change your mind.
Particularly if your views
are not the same as mine.
May you always
make room for playfulness.
It may just save your life.
And trust whatever makes your heart grow
cannot be a waste of time.

Wonderful

It may not make you money.
It may not even make sense.
But if it makes you happy
it is worth it in the end.
And it is worth it at the time,
and it deserves your very best.
And you are never too busy
to catch your breath.

Just as you cannot be in traffic
without being traffic,
life is not something
that you are stuck in
while it happens.
There is more in you
than you could possibly imagine.
The very fact that you exist
makes everything a bit more magic.

When it all feels too much
and there is little you can do,
may you still see the best in people
and may people include you.
May one thing match the gravity
of all you've ever done.
This wonderful reality:
the best is yet to come.

# Acknowledgements

Thank you Clive Birnie and Burning Eye, for being up for doing this third book with me, especially when the timeline was accelerated for the best of reasons.

Thank you Joel Baker, for making it all look so brilliant. I loved our joint exhibition and you are the kind of dad I want to be.

Thank you Harriet Evans, for helping it all make sense, and for such important editing notes as agreeing that *SSX Tricky* was the best game of all time.

Thank you Vicky McGuirk, for helping me piece myself back together when I thought that was no longer possible. Everyone should get therapy.

Thank you to anyone who has ever come to a gig, or shared my work with anyone else, or let me know that my poetry has meant something to them. You are the reason why I am able to do this.

Thank you to the Homeboy Cats, the Raclette Billionaires, the Handforth Parish Crew and the other various WhatsApp groups whose names definitely made sense at the time.[13] Let's hang out loads forever.

Thank you Mum and Dad, for valuing creativity over ownership, and helping me run a marathon every now and then.

Thank you Grace. You are the best and I love you.

13    Including but not limited to Living Legends, Fun People, Crazy Bats, Bangers and Mass, and the Dua Lipa Dream Team.